POIGNANT POESY

A COLLECTION OF POEMS

NILANJANA DAS BARMAN

To my God who sustained me through the storm

Contents

Contents

Preface

Poetry is distinctive from creative writing. Undoubtedly they share the same components of allegory and metaphor. However, poetry supersedes the boundaries of creative writing. Poetry can and is invariably taken out of context and made applicable to situations beyond its conception. My poems are no different in this regards than those of antiquity. Poetry has little geographical, temporal or cultural limitations.

The current volume is divided into five distinctive themes: On Society; On Emotions; On Moments; On Inevitability; On Finality. Before the reader is confounded with these titles or the content some light needs to be shed on the classification.

'On Society' deals with poetry that is inspired the contemporary world, the definitions of normalcy as perceived by the masses in spite of the individual struggles in coping with the plethora of expectations laid upon them for the sake of conformity.

'On Emotions' deal with an array of human feelings ranging from passion and love to guilt and detachment.

'On Moments' reflect a stream of consciousness limited to that moment. Some of these works are inspired by the works of others, literary, scientific, anecdotal. Each of these poems are different and include narrative as well as reflective poems.

'On Inevitability' consists of a group of poems dedicated to the passage of time and the changes that it brings about in life and in perspective. All of the poems deal with time, memory, death and beyond save for the last one which deals with reconciliation, something intrinsic to human relationships and society.

'On Finality' is a group of only three poems that deal with conclusion in its various forms, whether it be salvation of the spirit, freedom from one phase of life or the continuation of a cycle. This concludes my petite collection of verses.

Acknowledgements

I hereby acknowledge the people who have inspired me to write and inspired my poetry.

I thank my High School English Teacher, Late Jagadish Chandra Chakroborty, for his encouragement. Even though he is not in the world right now his encouragement continues to be with me.

I thank Jesus for standing by me when no one else did.

And I thank my family for accepting me as I am.

On Society

Human beings are social animals. We live within society and function as part of it. Our instincts are mellowed by the need for communication and communion. But being part of the society comes with consequences. Human society is less than ideal. There are subterfuge and lies at every conrner. Masks are worn universally. No one is honest, not intentionally, rather by default. Humans are bad judges of themselves, always being self-biased. On society deals with the trials and consequences of living within such a society.

At the same time we are the society. We determine the parameters that control social norms. We inspire fashion and instil morals and values. The failure of society is a personal failure. Hence the next seventeen poems are personal while being social.

1. Free

Stepping out:
One foot at a time;
Braving the new world
That recognizes you not,
Tells you that you're not enough.
You face fears calling you a coward,
Dreams calling you a dreamer:
One step at a time.
Stepping out isn't easy
But one step at a time
It must be done.
Looking through
A frost tinted window pane,
All that stands in the way:
The boy that told you, you were ugly,
That friend calling you stupid,
The wall you never dared to climb,
The door you never opened;
Looking through isn't easy:
The window taunts you,
A reflection of your
Scarred and battered face.
But you just have to open the window

And then face yourself;
Feeling free:
When the world is trying its best
To suffocate your every breath,
Clipping your wings at taking off,
Binding your tongue at the face off.
Feeling free is not at all easy.
But all you need
To not give up,
To not give in
To baseless shackles,
To overcome all the pointing fingers,
Is not a just a dream,
But a desire to try.

2. Real

It's assumed to be real.
The pain breaking you apart,
The joy of a brand new start,
The hope of gaining what's lost,
The warmth of crystallized frost:
It's all assumed to be real,
In a moment,
For a moment,
Till the moment is no more.
Suddenly you're not so sure.
But one assumption is real:
That life will endure.

3. Make Up

A little concealer to hide the bruise,
A tender sadness under the rouge,
Swollen lips behind the gloss,
Life is both silver and dross,
Brows plucked up in ardent care,
Against the skin painted fair,
Eyeshadow to hide the pain,
A little makeup and gone is the shame.
Hidden under the layer of clothes
The fear, anger, despair repose.
Wouldn't a tear their vanities expose?
But woe to the brunt of tainted desire,
Pity the wretched wings on fire
Vanity paints beauty into a liar.

4. The Obvious

Is it necessary to be obvious?
When the sun hits your eyes and you look away
Is it necessary to throw up your hand in defeat?
Life is not all about warning signals.
Life is all in its surprises.
Isn't it obvious
That every hope and every dream
Ends up in a rotten misery
Till something unexpected
Tugs a smile at the corner
Of battered down cracked lips?
When you laugh with a little tear shining
Right at the corner of your squinted eyes
Is it necessary to be obvious
That you haven't laughed in a while
That you haven't really lived
While keeping yourself busy,
Too busy to die?

5. When the World Stands Still

Could it matter really
If the world stood still?
What if the day never came,
And the night never left?
What if the sky never gave
The crimson hue of hope?
What if expectations never knocked
On a yet to be opened door?
Would life still be life,
With all its beginnings and endings?
Would death still be a death
With all its conjectures and uncertainties?
What if the world stopped in its track?
Would anyone stop to notice?

6. Darkness

• 9 •

It is not the darkness that scares me,

No more the empty room haunts,

No more the distant noises give the fright,

It is only the lies that taunt.

It's not the absence of light

That sends shivers down my spine,

It is the deceit of life:

It is the vanity of time.

7. Voiced Silence

• 10 •

Beyond a blur of chatter and chirping
The soul remains silent-
Reaching out in mute despair,
Holding on to vacant thoughts:
Some shrill some grave,
Some induced or borrowed,
Thoughts swimming in silence,
Words lost in the noise.

On Emotion

Emotions differentiate us from inanimate objects. The stones lying by the river too undergo wear and tear of ages, change and transform, like our lives. However they do not respond to the changes in laughter or tears. Our first reponse to any situation is borne out of our emotions. Some emotions we can overcome with discipline and some overpower our discipline, enslaving us.

While happiness and sorrow are emotions we experience, lust and helplessness are emotions that master us. The next fourteen poems focus on the various emotions and our response to them.

8. Lips

Devouring, panting,
Sighing or chanting,
Lips moving in silent prayer;
Friction from lip to lip
Or against empty air;
Emotions poured out,
From the heart sent forth,
A gesture of worship:
Humane or divine;
An expression of love-
From your lips to mine.

9. Unholy Prayers

Raging between two desires-
Fire tempting untamed fire;
Water sprinkled in vain
On stilled lakes of a silence, feigned.
Hope revealed in lustful eyes,
Lips parted in fearful goodbyes,,
Honeycomb drenched with lies
Blood pouring from restrained skies.
Two ends of a spectrum merging-
Passion, devotion, satisfaction surging;
To the seventh heaven and down to hell:
Sight, touch, taste and smell.
Exorcism of the sanest of minds,
Intoxication and pleasure combined,
Unholy prayers uttered on ravaged lips
And all of it- starts with a kiss.

10. Taste

It lures out the evil within us:
Saliva dripping in carnality;
One bite of our senses leads to-
One undeniable taste of sensuality!
The sweetness that fell the best
Before the blame was levied,
Before the elaborate plans,
All that mattered was the taste.
Juices running over a tongue
Reaching out for a bit more:
The serpent tasting around
For a morsel of ecstasy!
The venom cleverly hides,
A desire covertly divides;
Silent yet vociferous,
Righteous or malign.
It all comes back to the taste:
The gustation of desire,
The consummated fire,
To the gestation aspired.

11. The Unmade Bed

Crumpled sheets hiding an untold story,
Stained pillows holding a bucketful of pain,
Rolled blanket proxy for the absent shoulder,
Heaving heart and fictitious friction!
Daydreams substituting sound sleep:
A Sunday morning away from the church,
Thoughts wayward,
The distance chiming of the bell:
Calling me slowly back from hell.

12. Semblances

A shade:
Brown leaves,
Hanging by the tethers
To an old oak tree.
A shelter:
Of unspoken ambition,
Unfulfilled dreams,
Untimely passions:
Hollowing out
Howls of emptiness
To a semblance of security:
A mirage of promises,
And a climax of aspirations.
Death leaping down
On a rainbow trampoline:
Threatening with candy floss,
Shooting petals of crumpled roses,
Leaving stains of blood.
Passions extinguished in ashes:
Volcanic Ash,
Hiding the rumbling of an eruption
In heart-wrenching sobs:
A Pompeii in pieces.

The semblance of a home,
Broken into factions
Before it ever became a house:
Bricks scattered by stubbornness,
Mortar infested with silence,
A hope no more,
A dream no more!

13. Despair

Unshed Tears-
Wrecking havoc,
On wordless plea.
Bellicose passions
Muted in emptiness;
Turbulence was hidden behind
A lack of communication;
Rage bubbling with desire;
Silent complaints,
Patient fire;
A volcano
Erupting
Emotion:
Lava
Of
Passion.

14. Frozen

Frozen under a gaze;
In motion:
Craving for some semblance of animation!
In time:
Reaching out to the temporal vortex
A prison in its own right!
In ice:
A Sub-Zero cavern
Freezing molecules and moments alike!
The universe:
Drowned in the darkness of a black hole,
Steeped in the absolute zero of uncertainty!
Everything is frozen:
Refusing to thaw,
Refusing to change.
But heat seeps through in the end.

15. Submerged Truths

Lying under the surface
Of unspoken truths:
Lies
Sometimes vie
For social priority.
And I lie
In a midnight rage,
Holding on to
Shattered ideals.
All for a lie,
That society beckons
Everyone to tell.
Let life be hidden:
Behind half-truths,
Between deception:
Unshed Tears
Silent Sighs.

16. Note to Self

Don't cry,
Tears evaporate.
"Don't laugh,
Joy sublimates.
"Don't hope,
Expectations lie.
"Don't live,
We all have to die".
Note to self:
Stop giving a damn
Start appreciating your existence.

17. Old Us

Certain things never fade.
But we do,
Or the old version of us.
The sight, the smell,
The despair in our bones,
Beckoning us to hate,
Or forcing our love.
Imprints in our psyche
Renewing every night,
In a dream
Or a nightmare.
A pitiful affair,
We lose sight
Of where we are
Just because it's us.

18. Preferences

Whatever interests you
Is of little relevance.
Do you interest the spectators
Witnessing your life unfold?
Are your interests eccentric enough
To captivate a random stranger?
What do you prefer?
An existence under the surface,
Drawing in,
Drowning those who dare to wet their feet
In your cold, enticing current?
Darkness your greatest weapon,
Silence your greatest virtue,
Mystery your choicest allure
Rejuvenate never more.
Or do you wish to skim the surface,
Relishing the sunlight
Dance off the gentle ripples,
The lashing winds kiss your quivering skin,
Because it can,
Because you want to be reached out to?
Shallow, vain and naive,
Warm and vulnerable.

The world is an audience,
A gallery full of spectators,
Being entertained at your wounds,
Laughing inconsolably at your pain,
Internalising your laughter into hidden jokes,
Pointing fingers at your random mistakes-
Do you prefer to let them privy to your broken hopes and
ambitions?
Or do you simply play a game of role-playing,
Just to throw them off.
Preferences matter but the final choice is all.

19. Pain Drug

The numbing is good for emotions:
Detaching the mind to release the flesh,
Counting invisible stars on a bare ceiling.
It's amazing how pain can make you feel alive
When pleasures leave you feeling empty;
When desires exploit and dreams torment-
It's the pain that doesn't let you forget to breathe,
To heave.
The piercing pain, the searing burn,
Tossed and turned;
Hope to suffocate in the midst of despair,
Overwhelming,
The fear is only fair.
Yet all that matters is the pain,
Propagating through the veins,
Not letting the sorrow through.
The floodgates of emotions restricted:
Skin biting,
Scars and bruises,
Superficial!
The skin protects the flesh.
The flesh protects the heart.
Pain is all I feel,

Because if I don't-
Pain rips me apart.

Because if I don't-
Pain rips me apart.

20. Where is Love?

Travelling for an aeon
And still searching:
What uncharted territory
Left unturned?
The crevices of darkness,
The precipice of glory,
The seat of illumination,
Love lays beyond imagination.
A concept,
A gesture,
Drenched in two-thousand-year-old blood
That refuses to dry.
Washing through-
Crimson purer than white;
Death becomes the one who loves.
Where then is love itself?
The pangs of labour,
The agony and torment,
Hopes and dreams,
All clouded by
A bunch of expectations:
A life yet to be lived-
At the price of lives voluntarily forfeited.

The search goes on.
The mirror stares still,
Narcissism smiles content,
Before the glass is shattered:
Before the world comes crashing down.
You can never love yourself enough.
The question repeating in your mind,
Over and over again,
Where is love?

21. Communication

So easy and difficult to convey:
Words bubbling from a quiet conscience-
Holding on to a possibility
Making way towards the incredible.
A path from me to you:
Holding an image-
Of my comprehension;
A day, a moment:
Immortalized,
Digitalized,
Embedded in bits;
Bits have torn from reality to virtual,
Projecting it to the universe,
In a universally accepted form.
An idea, a thought,
All transferred,
All translated;
A lifeless machine
Acting as a lifeline
As my heart beats within
Reaching out.
Written lines,
Spoken words,

Frozen gestures,
All turned to waves,
Disturbances,
In the fabric of reality.

On Moments

Moments stand out from the many events of life. We describe most as mundane, some as extraordinary but only a few as inspirational. These seven poems have been inspired by the works of other writers and poets.

The Quantum Field of Existence has been inspired by a poem titled 'A Happy Little Speck in the Illuminatarium of Time' is a poem I read on an online poetry writing platform. In the course of my involvement with that platform I had built a rapport with the poet of the said poem. That was many years back and I regret to state two things- I lost touch with the person and I have forgotten the original poem that inspired this.

Minkowski Space was something inspired from my study of Relativistic Physics.

Apocalypse was inspired by 'The Day of the Doctor' the 50th Anniversary special in the longest running Television Series in History- Doctor Who.

Tom Riddle's Choice is evidently a nod to Harry Potter, the movies, not the stories per se.

Vampire Lust is all about L.J.Smith's Vampire Diaries.

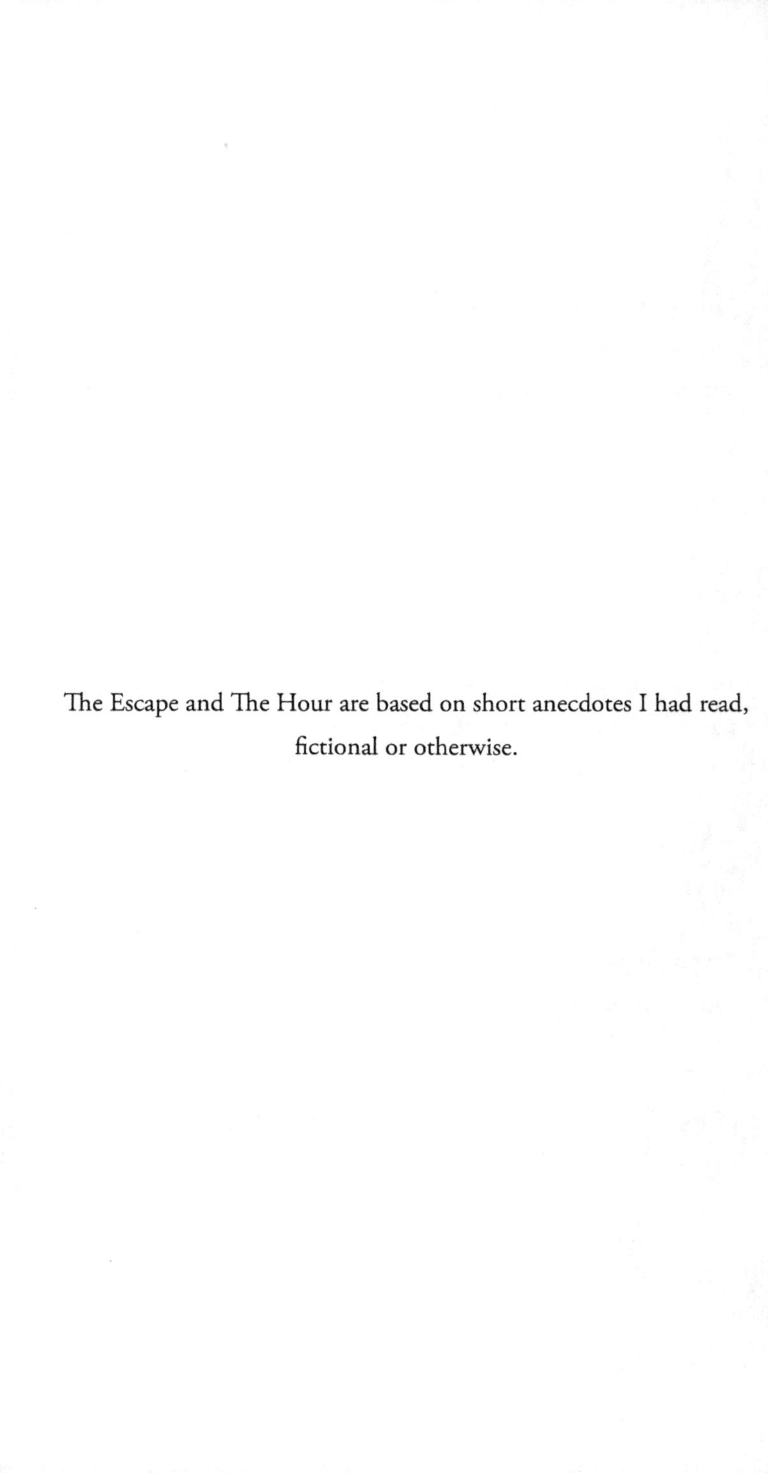

The Escape and The Hour are based on short anecdotes I had read, fictional or otherwise.

22. The Quantum Field of Existence

A Ripple

In the fabric of reality;

A count

In the probability of existence;

I sometimes wish that I was not so insignificant.

Defined by parameters

Beyond me;

Measured by the influences

That shaped me;

A purpose confined to

Cause and effect;

Magnitude

Measured in reaction.

If I were not strung

To a sequence of events,

I could be my own person:

A name that is written in stone.

But even the stone disappears,

Phasing in and out of reality,
As time flows,
From one space to another.
Hope remains,
Not defined,
Not expressed,
Simply existing.

23. Minkowski Space

When the past is hurled
Towards a future that is muddled,
And when the present is simply
Yet to start taking place,
Life is nothing
But a bunch of coordinates,
In a four-dimensional,
Minkowski space.
When silence is golden,
When music is molten,
When voices drift out of old,
Memories are nothing
But random points
In the continuum
Of space-time
Fourfold.
When vision is trained
On a goal unseen,
When the heart is trained
On a future
Evergreen,
Olden and new,
Numerous and few,

Qualities are strewn,
A string of possibilities
In a theoretical space.

24. The Escape

The water was still:
Not a ripple, not a bubble!
Was it sheer skill?
Did someone hear a shuffle,
In the watery grave
Of a talent so young?
The audience was stunned!
Just a trick
To those afloat,
Just a victory
For the magician to gloat.

25. The Hour

The girl smiled at the man who smiled back:
The wrinkles in his face saw the light in her eyes;
Both standing at the corner of the road-
One in an expensive suit the other in threadbare robes.
Nothing tied them, not language not creed,
They both stood beyond selfishness and greed;
She had flowers in her hands filled with thorns,
He had a desire spent and hopes forlorn.
A little bit of money widened her smile;
A bunch of flowers made his gesture worthwhile;
And as the flower girl went off to a bite she craved,
The man placed the flowers beside his dead wife's grave.
And the tears that threatened at the hint of a smile
No longer seemed redundant, nor sobs seemed too wild;
And as the tears poured life took seed,
In an hour of solitude, grief is freed.

26. Apocalypse

The world has ended

And it feels like a dream.

Moments:

That is all it takes,

A flash of lightning

And everything is nothing

The world has ended.

It was just moments ago:

There was laughter,

There were tears,

There was a possibility,

Hidden in unexplored potential,

In untapped resources,

Till all was wiped clean.

A new beginning.

The world has ended,

And Revelations abound:

The trumpet sounds.

No more waiting,

No more hope,

No more chances,
No more.
The war has ended,
Yet Gallifrey falls no more.

27. Tom Riddle's Choice

"Inspired by 'Harry Potter and the Half Blood Prince'"

Immortality, invincibility,

It's tempting

Is it easy to break or be broken

Beyond obscurity

A life that goes on

Beyond roots, beyond form.

That or a life that survives

Grovelling amongst ignominy.

What is life but every moment lived?

What is death but the fear of it?

In reality a moment of non-existence

In theory the sound of impending oblivion.

Remove the fear and remove death.

Broken to be whole:

What is murder, homicide, manslaughter?

A life extinguished,

Human machinery damaged,

A clink in the chain of dependence,

All falling back upon mutual mortality.

Is it really easy to be mortal,

To face death every day
Among dear ones and quaint acquaintances?
Is it easy to know your vulnerability,
Be aware of the ache of insecurity
Gnawing at your weaknesses
Till you surrender to every invisible enemy?
Who am I? Who are we?
A number in the probability of life.
The one who conquers death
Conquers fear and conquers strife.
Sacrifice it is, few deaths to save one;
Or is it one death to save all:
Once for all?
But that is absurd,
The probability next to none
And so rises Voldemort!

28. Vampire Lust

It's the hunger that drives me crazy-
The deep-seated lust for blood:
Drawing out from the recesses of your psyche,
That no one else could search;
I throb for the depth of you,
The length and the breadth of you,
Encompassing in a bone-crushing hug.
My lips are parched from emptiness,
The soullessness of my subconscious self,
Hankering to absorb you;
Fill me from within, extending without,
Withering away in your absence.
Precious blood:
Dripping down a weathered wooden cross,
Burning a mark through my skin,
Marked for the butchering,
A stake through my heart,
Borne on torn flesh,
Oozing out with life,
Eternal life.
Word mere words,
Yet life-giving, soul quenching,
Manna dripping with hope,

A second chance at a beating heart
Whether mine or yours.
Fill me now, into dry withered bones
Aged with death, time and loss.
Drench me with life, ruddy wet drops;
Free my existence from the worldly strife
The lust that keeps me going,
The hope that keeps me scoffing,
The words that keep me awake,
The death that keeps me sleeping:
Soulless, heartless, lifeless,
Fangs sinking into innocence,
Thirsty for life:
Tears of blood, bloodshot eyes
Vampire lust.

On Inevitability

Inevitability talks about all that cannot be avoided on earth. From the passage of time to the temptation of lust and ending in the permanance of death. Despite my Christian beliefs, these poems tend to focus on the now and not the hereafter. It is focussed at the reader's perception of reality.

29. Passage of Years

It begins and it ends,
And between is a process to survive,
To walk into the next day
With a troubled head held high;
Surviving the darkness of the night,
Grappling through the morning haze
Fighting for a morsel and a loaf
A hope and a dream to sustain.
It begins with pomp:
A resolution to proclaim;
It ends with a yawn:
Tired eyes,
Waiting for a tomorrow,
Waiting for an unknown;
The unknown comes
Only to leave again,
And through the passage of time
A year is here and it is not.

30. Union

We all try to better ourselves:
Man to Superman, soul to supersoul!
We are all searching for our better half,
Striving every day to become a whole.
The mind merges in conversation,
The soul emerges in adoration,
Flesh joins and separates
Desire blossoms and permeates.
Day-in, day-out we roam about and creep,
The union we seek surreal and deep,
Never realizing our eternal groom
Is preparing for us a transcendental room.
At his call, the clouds shall part,
To be with him souls shall depart,
And through the perfect sacrifice
Union shall rain in fire and ice.

31. A Shallow Grave

Every day we dig ourselves
A shallow little grave.
In every offence and lie,
In every bitter goodbye,
And it gets deeper still,
Till the tears and curses fill,
Our way down to the blaze.
Misery follows,
And the gnashing of teeth,
When we are buried in cold hearts
More than six feet deep.

32. Tomorrow

A nagging preoccupation,
An addiction without a narcotic,
No psychedelics required,
Only hope and dreams:
Is positivity really a good thing?
Is time really in the passage?
A journey through the events-
A four-dimensional line with one direction:
Towards death and disaster,
Or life and immortality.
Tomorrow is a question mark-
Drowned in probability.

33. On Time and Memory

Moments come and moments go
Memories vacillate in between.
Life holds on to reason:
Certain impossible rules!
All logic crumbling at the precipice:
Holding on to a past that never was,
Hoping for a future that never is to be.
The memories of a hope
Not worth remembering,
Worming its way into a mind
Reluctant to let go
Of pain and pleasure,
In indiscriminate amounts.
Time moves on,
Life moves on,
Yet in the midst of all,
Stagnation-
Is what we become.

34. Fragments

In art and amnesia
We lose ourselves.
The strokes of colour
Old, familiar, and unknown;
In the crooked uneven lines
That outlines a well-loved home,
Reduced to a silhouette
Of once conquered dreams.
A plan that has gone wrong,
Desires floundered in deceit,
Eyes remain a vivid memory,
Stirring passions uncalled
Yet the face passes in a blur.
Beautiful and serene
The fragment of a memory
Holding peace
In a piece
Of simplicity.

35. Kingdom of Heaven

Desire and dreams,
And the all too familiar stench-
Of rotting corpses,
In the folds of the subconscious;
The soot from the burning cinders,
Of conscience killed in abandon-
Set upon a funeral pyre
Of compromises and adjustments-
Guilt well masked,
In the intoxicated eyes of exuberance-
Shame be upon you deceit,
The harlot to all things inhuman,
Mistress to lust, bearer of woe,
Seeded with guile and allure:
A pleasant smile on your face,
Inviting ruby red lips,
The venomous kiss of sin
Enveloped in a conscience,
Beaten down, raped of innocence,
Murdered with temptation,
Envelop me in the numbness of your pain.
Punishment come and in me reign;
In your meagre touch of salvation,

Be my Kingdom of heaven.

36. Flowers

Flowers: precious white,
The harbinger of life,
With nectar in it blossoms
And secrets in its bosom
Delicate and shy;
See the bees that fly
In secret adoration,
Owning to temptation,
And the plundering kiss,
Intentions amiss,
Delicate hues wither,
Like torn white feathers:
And the bird stoops low,
Refusing to let go,
But the blossom must fall,
For the tree to stand tall.
Trampled underfoot,
It dies for the greater good
And till the next morn
The flower is but gone.

37. Loyalty

Everything is up for sale nowadays-
Come and buy pleasure a-plenty.
All it costs is your peace of mind:
A broken trust,
A look that says 'guilty'.
Whose guilt is it?
Whose shame do you bear?
It's the bed you made that you lie in.
Tangled in lies that make it tempting-
The forbidden fruit of desire,
Setting senses on fire.
It's my sin and yours,
Caught between sheets,
Stained with blood and tears:
A little greasepaint
To mask all the regrets,
Camouflage that reeks of duplicity.
Promises kept were, one day,
Sweet;
Now it's just a pain,
But life with a little pain-
It's easier, isn't it?
But still, trust is not for sale.

I wonder if my eyes would wander
If it wasn't forbidden to look away,
But now it matters no longer,
There are cracks in the wall
Where our home once lay.
Let's swear by one another,
Because when the adventure ends
It's all that remains:
The flesh of my flesh
And a life we complicate
Into a mess.
Come back sweet love
For promises to keep:
The ocean of life chaffed and roared,
It's high tide and the boat is ready to sail:
Ride the waves and let us both go home.

On Finality

The last three poems of this collection all speak of the end in one way or another. Whether that end becomes a new beginning depends on us and not on our circumstances.

38. Freedom in Captivity

I was a free bird:
Always, most of the time,
When my irrational fears
Did not hold me captive,
When my undying hope
Kept me waiting in a limbo,
Then you came to put me in a cage;
I flapped my wings in defiance,
I clawed at the walls of security,
I pecked the pillars of submission,
I cried my heart out for Adventures,
Till finally, the cage opened;
And one brief look back
Towards the walls of security,
At the pillars of submission,
Made my heart lurch with longing
For the cage of my safety
And that's where forever be:
My land of Canaan,
My fountain of Eden,
My dream of forever.

39. Finally

Finally:

Wings are set free,

Broken hearts joined.

Finally:

A canvas is painted in

A rainbow hue

Of a summer Glee.

Finally;

The world is silent

In self-satiation

In the post-coital bliss:

Of intelligence and intoxication.

Finally:

A crumpled flower is

Salvaged in

An artist's imagination,

An attempted Resurrection,

A song of satisfaction,

Singing:

...

Finally.

40. The End

The curtain fell,
The lights were put out,
The tissue papers were brought forth,
Applauses were heard among the wiping of tears,
Sniffling of sighs, a revelation of fears,
The actor bowed, curtsied and sighed,
"At last the end has come"
The audience left,
The characters had realized their destinies,
To live, to die, to grow old, narrate lies,
The actor tires, greasepaint wiped, parted ways,
The end has come on the last day,
And the troupe must thus break,
"At last the end has come".
A week and a month,
The rehearsals in full swing:
Cast restructured, actors regrouped,
Characters reborn, recast in new suits,
A new day and a new beginning:
Alas! The end never comes.

About The Author

Nilanjana Das Barman, (earlier writing under the pseudonym of Anavah Moses) is a Physics teacher from Kolkata. She has two published novels, eleven volumes of poetry, three Christian devotionals and two novellas available on amazon. Her writing has been featured in the international literary journal, "The Wingless Dreamer" in its 2021 BIPOC issue. When she is not writing or explaining Newton's Laws of Motion you can find her with a brush in hand.